K

Learn to Knit
Cables!

Photography by John Cranford
Book Design and Editing by Lee Meredith

Printed in the United States of America
First Printing, 2021

ISBN 978-1-62767-284-9

Versa Press, Inc.

800-447-7829
www.versapress.com

Contents

Hover your phone camera over the QR code for:

- » Video tutorials
- » More photo tutorials
- » More cable patterns
- » All the yarn and tools you need!

(knitpicks.com/learning-center/knit-bits-learn-to-cable)

What Are Cables?

See how they look like stitches are twisted around or over/under each other? That's because that's exactly what's happening! The stitches are knit just like any other knit stitch, but their positions are moved around on the needle to make the twists or braids.

Cables like the ones here are made with knit stitches, and are surrounded on each side by purl stitches (Reverse Stockinette Stitch) to make them pop off the fabric. Cable patterns can involve different combinations of knits and purls, but the twisting concept is always the same.

For this swatch, all the cables were worked in one color, and then the top bit was knit with two colors to better illustrate what's happening. Normally, cables are not worked in two colors (they can be, but it's more advanced) so the colors are only to help you see the front/back or left/right stitches.

All cables are twisted either to the right or to the left, and for this to happen, the first stitch(es) are brought either to the back or to the front of the next stitch(es).

Note: The yarn used in the tutorials is Twill!

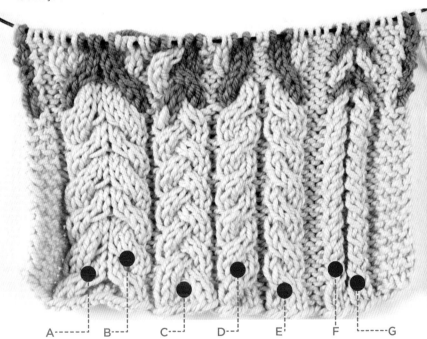

A------- B--- C--- D--- E F '------G

A) Switch between 2-over-3 Right Cable & 3-over-2 Right Cable every fourth row; **B)** Switch between 2-over-3 Left Cable & 3-over-2 Left Cable every fourth row; **C)** Switch between (2-over-2 Left Cable, K2) & (K2, 2-over-2 Right Cable) every other row; **D)** 2-over-2 Right Cable every fourth row; **E)** 2-over-2 Left Cable every fourth row; **F)** 1-over-1 Right Twist every other row; **G)** 1-over-1 Left Twist every other row.

TWIST DIRECTION

See what direction a twist is going by following the direction of the twist. If a cable is twisting up (towards the needle or the live stitches) to the left, it's a **Left Cable**; up to the right, it's a **Right Cable**.

Different patterns may label cables as Right/Left *or* Back/Front twists. So this is good to know:

> » **Right = Back**
> » **Left = Front**

This means if the **first** stitches are held to the **back**, the cable will twist to the **right**, and if the **first** stitches are held to the **front**, the cable will twist to the **left**.

In other words, if the first stitches are traveling in back, the next stitches must be in front, traveling **from left to right**, making a **right** twist; if the first stitches are traveling in front, that means they are going over the front of the other stitches, moving **from right to left**, making a **left** twist.

If this isn't making sense, try following the tutorials to knit some cables then come back here and see if it clicks!

Another terminology note: Some patterns may name cables in different ways, such as **4-stitch Cable** instead of **2-over-2 Cable**. Once you understand how cables work, you can read instructions for a cable and know what's meant to happen, regardless of label.

The Tutorials

1-OVER-1 TWISTS

1-over-1 cables are also called twists, **Right Twist** (RT) and **Left Twist** (LT). You'll be shown here how to work them with a cable needle, as a cable introduction.

Generally these would not require a cable needle. If you're knitting a pattern with lots of twists (like the *Bowline Hat*), visit **the QR code link** on page 3 for tutorials on twists made three different ways without cable needles, or you can use the same no-cable-needle methods as for bigger cables.

BASIC CABLES

Next you'll make a **Left Cable** and a **Right Cable**, using 2-over-2 cables to learn—the same methods work for any stitch counts.

WITHOUT A CABLE NEEDLE

Once you understand how cables are made, this skill will make cable-heavy projects go much more quickly, and allow you to make a cable anywhere, anytime!

This method is easier and more risk-free with a "sticky" wool or a somewhat rugged yarn, rather than a slippery fiber like silk or alpaca.

GENERAL NOTE

All slips are always purl-wise unless otherwise noted. That means the stitch moves across from one needle to another without twisting in either direction.

Tools There are different kinds of **cable needles (CNs)**; the curved kind pictured in the tutorials or the U-shaped kinds tend to stay out of your way as you work more easily than the straight kind, so those are good ones to learn with. Once you are familiar with making cables, you can see what cable needle shape you prefer, and you can even use a plain double pointed needle (great in a pinch, if you're out somewhere and forgot to bring a cable needle!). Your cable needle does not need to be the same size/diameter as your knitting needle—smaller works just fine.

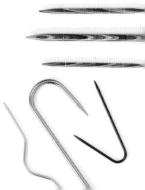

LT (1-over-1 Left Cable)

1-over-1 cables are also called twists: Right Twist (RT) and Left Twist (LT), since they can be worked different ways (see previous page). We'll be working them here with a cable needle as a simple introduction to how cable needles and cable knitting in general work.

Left Twist: Step 1

Slip the first stitch onto the cable needle (purl-wise, as always).

Left Twist: Step 2

Hold the cable needle to the front.

Left Twist: Step 3

Knit the next 1 stitch from the knitting needle.

Left Twist: Step 4

Grab the cable needle and hold it in your hand to knit the stitch from it.

Left Twist: Step 5

Knit that stitch, just like a regular knit stitch.

Left Twist: Done!

The first stitch was crossed over the second stitch, traveling in front, twisting to the left.

RT (1-over-1 Right Cable)

Right Twist: Step 1

Slip the first 1 stitch to the cable needle, then hold it to the back of your work, behind the needles.

Right Twist: Step 2

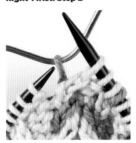

Knit the next stitch from the left needle while holding the cable needle in the back. Then pick the cable needle back up and hold it up to knit the stitch from it.

Right Twist: Step 3

Knit that back stitch directly off the cable needle.

Right Twist: Done!

By holding the first stitch to the back, you've just made a right twisting cable!

Now that you know the concept of how cables are worked, turn the page to do the same thing with more stitches!

A 2-over-2 cable is made with 4 stitches total, 2 held to either the front or back, over or under the other 2, to make the left or right cable twist. It works the same way with any number of stitches.

All cables are basically worked the same way, so once you grasp the concept and learn how to do basic cable twists, you'll know what you need to tackle your first cabled project.

Don't worry about mastering the no-cable-needle techniques until you feel up to it; they will be there waiting for you when you're ready!

Left Cable (LC)

These will all be shown as 2-over-2 cables, but the same steps apply to any numbers of stitches. For Left Cables, the first set of stitches goes in front, the second set in back. For a 3-over-1 Left Cable, the *front stitches* start as the first 3, *back stitches* as the last 1.

Left Cable: Ready!

Those first 2 (blue) stitches will twist in front of the second 2 (gold) stitches to make the left twist.

Left Cable: Step 1

Slip the first set of stitches (front stitches) to the cable needle, and let the needle drop to the front.

Left Cable: Step 2

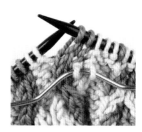

Work the next set of stitches (back stitches) from the knitting needle.

Left Cable: Step 3

Pick up the cable needle, and hold it up to knit the stitches from it.

Left Cable: Step 4

Knit across the (front) stitches from the cable needle.

Left Cable: Done!

The stitches have flipped places; gold stitches now to the right, blue stitches twisted in front to the left. On the next row, work across those stitches normally.

LC without a Cable Needle

Left Cable, no CN: Step 1

For a left cable without a cable needle, start by slipping ALL the stitches (in this 2-over-2 cable that's 4 stitches) over to the right-hand knitting needle.

Left Cable, no CN: Step 2

Bring the left-hand needle across the front and stick it through the front stitches, the right set of stitches on the right-hand needle.

Left Cable, no CN: Step 3

Work the next two steps smoothly and carefully: With your left hand holding your knitting in place, slip the right-hand needle out of ALL the cable stitches...

Left Cable, no CN: Step 4

...then slip it immediately back into the loose back stitches. (Those stitches will only be loose for a second, as the needle slips out and then right back in.)

Left Cable, no CN: Step 5

Slip the back stitches from the right-hand needle onto the left-hand needle. Now all unworked cable stitches are ready to knit, in the new correct twisted order.

Left Cable, no CN: Step 6

Work the first set of stitches (the back stitches), then knit the next set of stitches (the front stitches). (When finished, it will look exactly like *Done!* on page 8.)

Right Cable (RC)

These will all be shown as 2-over-2 cables, but the same steps apply to any numbers of stitches. For Right Cables, the first set of stitches goes in back, the second set in front. For a 3-over-1 Right Cable, the *front stitches* start as the last 3, *back stitches* as the first 1.

Right Cable: Ready!

Those first (gold) stitches will twist in back of the second (blue) stitches to make the right twist.

Right Cable: Step 1

Slip the first set of stitches (back stitches) to the cable needle, then let it drop to the back of your work.

Right Cable: Step 2

Knit the next set of stitches (front stitches) from the knitting needle. (The cable needle just hangs in back.)

Right Cable: Step 3

Grab the cable needle and hold it up to knit from it.

Right Cable: Step 4

Work across the (back) stitches from the cable needle.

Right Cable: Done!

The stitches have flipped places; blue stitches now in front to the right, gold stitches twisted to the left. On the next row, work across those stitches normally.

RC without a Cable Needle

Right Cable, no CN: Step 1

For a right cable without a cable needle, bring the right-hand needle across the front of your work and through the second set of stitches (the front stitches).

Right Cable, no CN: Step 2

Work the next two steps smoothly and carefully: Holding your knitting firmly in your right hand, slip the left-hand needle out of ALL the cable stitches...

Right Cable, no CN: Step 3

...then slip it immediately back into the loose back stitches. (Those stitches will only be loose for a second, as the needle slips out and then right back in.)

Step 3 continued...

What used to be the left stitches are twisted in front, on the right-hand needle; what used to be the right stitches are twisted in back, on the left-hand needle.

Right Cable, no CN: Step 4

Slip the (front) stitches from the right-hand needle back over to the left-hand needle. Now all the stitches are ready to work in their new cable twisted order.

Right Cable, no CN: Step 5

Knit the first set of stitches (the front stitches), then work the next set of stitches (the back stitches). (When finished, it will look exactly like *Done!* on page 10.)

More Complex Cables

BRAIDED CABLES

This braid-style cable (shown to the right) is made by twisting 6 stitches total as 2-over-2 cables, one cable twist per right-side row. To work this cable: on a right-side row, work the first set of 4 stitches as a 2-over-2 Left Cable, then knit the last 2 stitches normally; on the following right-side row, knit the first 2 stitches normally, then work the next 4 stitches as a 2-over-2 Right Cable. The way the stitches are cabled around each other is just like a 3-strand braid (think hair braid!): twist the outer stitches up over the center stitches, first on one side, then the other side, and just keep repeating.

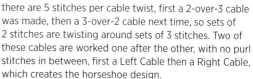

ASYMMETRICAL HORSESHOE

To the left is an example of asymmetrical cables—there are 5 stitches per cable twist, first a 2-over-3 cable was made, then a 3-over-2 cable next time, so sets of 2 stitches are twisting around sets of 3 stitches. Two of these cables are worked one after the other, with no purl stitches in between, first a Left Cable then a Right Cable, which creates the horseshoe design.

PURLING THE BACK STITCHES

The most common variation you'll find is a very simple one: purling the stitches in the back instead of knitting them. For this, you'll work the cable exactly as the instructions show (either with or without a cable needle) but purl the stitches held to the back, which are the first set of stitches on a left twist, or the last set of stitches on a right twist.

EXTRA COMPLEX CABLES

Most cables you encounter, no matter how complex, will be worked using the same methods as the ones we've just learned, with a set of stitches (could be 2, or 3 or 4...) twisting either right or left over another set of stitches. Some complex cables might have an extra step, or even use two cable needles with more than two sets of stitches—you'll see some of these kinds of twists in the *Tuckamore Wrap* pattern. You can follow even these tricky cables by working each step of the pattern as written.

Another complex type of cable you may find in some patterns is one that incorporates an increase or decrease into the cable stitches. If you know how to work the increase or decrease, and you know how to make the cable, then you'll be able to follow the steps and make the pattern! You'll encounter some of these in the *Bowline Hat* pattern.

Cable Tips & Tricks

Here are a couple of extra things for if you're not working from a pattern. These tips are unimportant if you're following a pattern, as the pattern will tell you exactly how to work each row. However, if you want to experiment with your own cable ideas, read on for a better understanding of the basic "rules" of cable construction.

CABLE SPACING

First, the general rule of thumb for how often to work a cable twist is: work as many rows are there are stitches in the cable for each repeat. Round down for an odd number of stitches (unless you're working in the round, in which case there's no reason you need to work cables only on odd or even numbered rounds). Here are some examples:

» For a 1-over-1 cable, there are 2 cable sts involved, so work the cable twist on every 2nd row, which means every RS row.

» For a 2-over-2 cable, there are 4 cable sts involved, so work the cable twist on every 4th row. This means after working a cable row, work 1 WS row, then 1 RS row, then 1 more WS row; work the cable row on the next RS row.

» For a 3-over-3 cable, there are 6 cable sts involved, so work the cable twist on every 6th row. So work 2 plain RS rows between cable rows, making 6 rows total in the pattern repeat (3 right-side, 3 wrong-side).

» For an asymmetrical 2-over-3 / 3-over-2 cable, round down to 4 sts and work the cable every 4th row. Or you may want to try rounding up and working the cable every 6th row, and see the difference between the two options—you might prefer one over the other.

» For the braided cable on page 12, a cable is worked on every RS row because they switch sides. So the first kind of cable—2-over-2 Left over the first 4 sts—is only being worked every 4th row, and the other cable, worked over the last 4 sts, is being worked on the opposite RS rows, also every 4th row.

CABLE GAUGE

The other tip to keep in mind is that cables pull in the knitting significantly, as the stitches pull across left and right to twist, so adding cables to a project will significantly affect your stitch gauge. For example, if you know that a hat in the same yarn weight that fits you well has 100 stitches around in stockinette, but you want to add some cables to it, you'll need to cast on more than 100 stitches to compensate for the change in gauge and elasticity.

Try adding half as many stitches as there are in the cables; for example, if you're adding five 2-over-2 cables (which use 4 stitches each), that's 20 stitches total in all the cables, so add 10 extra stitches. This math may or may not be perfect, depending on your yarn, density, specific cables ... so pay attention as you work, measure your cable pattern gauge as needed, and do what you need to do to get the results you want!

Coho Cowl
By Allison Griffith

Finished Measurements
52 (24)" circumference × 8 (13.25)"
height (sample is 52" size)

Yarn
Swish™ (worsted weight, 100% Fine
Superwash Merino Wool; 110 yards/50g):
Haystack Heather 28653, 4 skeins

Needles
US 7 (4.5 mm) straight or circular needles
(24" or longer), or size to obtain gauge

Notions
Yarn Needle
Stitch Markers (optional)
Cable Needle

Gauge
27 sts and 28 rows = 4" in Cable Pattern,
blocked
1 Cable Pattern rep = 12 sts and 28
rows = 1.75" and 4" (gauge is not
crucial, but it will affect finished
size and yardage requirements)

The Coho Cowl is the perfect project to practice and perfect your cable technique. Featuring six different cable crosses and a fully written and charted, easily-memorized repeat pattern, this project will take you from beginner to intermediate (or beyond!).

This pattern includes two sizes: a deep and narrow cowl for maximum snuggliness and a longer, looser cowl, perfect for doubling up around your neck on cool days.

This cowl is worked flat, beginning at one short end. Once the cowl is worked to the desired length, the cast on and bind off edges are seamed together, creating a cylindrical cowl.

Chart is worked flat; read RS rows (odd numbers) from right to left, and WS rows (even numbers) from left to right. Cable crosses are only worked on RS rows.

Markers are optional and may be placed as indicated to help keep track of pattern.

2/2 RC (Cable 2 over 2 Right)
Sl2 to CN, hold in back; K2, K2 from CN.

2/2 LC (Cable 2 over 2 Left)
Sl2 to CN, hold in front; K2, K2 from CN.

2/1 RPC (Cable 2 over 1 Right, Purl back)
Sl1 to CN, hold in back; K2, P1 from CN.

2/1 LPC (Cable 2 over 1 Left, Purl back)
Sl2 to CN, hold in front; P1, K2 from CN.

2/2 RPC (Cable 2 over 2 Right, Purl back)
Sl2 to CN, hold in back; K2, P2 from CN.

2/2 LPC (Cable 2 over 2 Left, Purl back)
Sl2 to CN, hold in front; P2, K2 from CN.

COHO CABLE PATTERN

Row 1 (RS): K3, (P4, 2/2 RC, P4) 4 (7) times, K3.

Row 2 (WS): K7, P4, K4, (K4, P4, K4) 3 (6) times, K3.

Row 3: K3, (P3, 2/1 RPC, 2/1 LPC, P3) 4 (7) times, K3.

Row 4: K6, P2, K2, P2, K3, (K3, P2, K2, P2, K3) 3 (6) times, K3.

Row 5: K3, (P1, 2/2 RPC, P2, 2/2 LPC, P1), 4 (7) times, K3.

Row 6: K4, P2, K6, P2, K1, (K1, P2, K6, P2, K1) 3 (6) times, K3.

Row 7: K3, (2/1 RPC, P6, 2/1 LPC) 4 (7) times, K3.

Row 8: K3, (P2, K8, P2) 4 (7) times, K3.

Row 9: K5, (P8, 2/2 LC) 3 (6) times, P8, K5.

Row 10: K3, (P2, K8, P2) 4 (7) times, K3.

Row 11: K3, (2/1 LPC, P6, 2/1 RPC) 4 (7) times, K3.

Row 12: K4, P2, K6, P2, K1, (K1, P2, K6, P2, K1) 3 (6) times, K3.

Row 13: K3, (P1, 2/2 LPC, P2, 2/2 RPC, P1) 4 (7) times, K3.

Row 14: K6, P2, K2, P2, K3, (K3, P2, K2, P2, K3) 3 (6) times, K3.

Row 15: K3, (P3, K2, P2, K2, P3) 4 (7) times, K3.

Row 16: K6, P2, K2, P2, K3, (K3, P2, K2, P2, K3) 3 (6) times, K3.

Row 17: K3, (P1, 2/2 RPC, P2, 2/2 LPC, P1) 4 (7) times, K3.

Row 18: K4, P2, K6, P2, K1, (K1, P2, K6, P2, K1) 3 (6) times, K3.

Row 19: K3, (2/1 RPC, P6, 2/1 LPC) 4 (7) times, K3.

Row 20: K3, (P2, K8, P2) 4 (7) times, K3.

Row 21: K5, (P8, 2/2 LC) 3 (6) times, P8, K5.

Row 22: K3, (P2, K8, P2) 4 (7) times, K3.

Row 23: K3, (2/1 LPC, P6, 2/1 RPC) 4 (7) times, K3.

Row 24: K4, P2, K6, P2, K1, (K1, P2, K6, P2, K1) 3 (6) times, K3.

Row 25: K3, (P1, 2/2 LPC, P2, 2/2 RPC, P1) 4 (7) times, K3.
Row 26: K6, P2, K2, P2, K3, (K3, P2, K2, P2, K3) 3 (6) times, K3.
Row 27: K3, (P3, 2/1 LPC, 2/1 RPC, P3) 4 (7) times, K3.
Row 28: K7, P4, K4, (K4, P4, K4) 3 (6) times, K3.

Directions

Loosely CO 54 (90) sts.
Setup Row (WS): K3, PM, K4, P4, K4, PM, (K4, P4, K4, PM) 3 (6) times, K3.

Work Coho Cable Pattern (from written rows or chart) Rows 1–28. If working from chart, rep red boxed sts 3 (6) times across each row.

If using optional markers: Ms will fall between reps. On Rows 9 and 21, remove Ms when working cable crosses, and replace them back in centers of cable sts after cables have been worked.

Cont in pattern until 13 (6) reps of Rows 1–28 have been completed, or until reaching desired cowl length, ending final rep with Row 27 (RS).

BO all sts. Break yarn, leaving a tail at least 24 (36)" long.

FINISHING

Use a yarn needle and the yarn tail to seam the CO edge and BO edge together, being careful not to twist, and doing your best to match up the cables. Use Mattress Stitch, but worked horizontally instead of vertically, so that the needle is passing under the two strands of each knit stitch, instead of under the two bars between sts.

Weave in ends, wash, and block to measurements.

COHO CABLE PATTERN

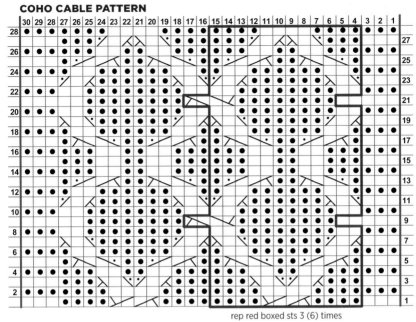

rep red boxed sts 3 (6) times

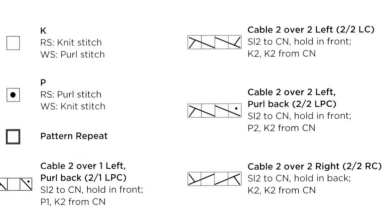

K
RS: Knit stitch
WS: Purl stitch

P
RS: Purl stitch
WS: Knit stitch

Pattern Repeat

**Cable 2 over 1 Left,
Purl back (2/1 LPC)**
Sl2 to CN, hold in front;
P1, K2 from CN

**Cable 2 over 1 Right,
Purl back (2/1 RPC)**
Sl1 to CN, hold in back;
K2, P1 from CN

Cable 2 over 2 Left (2/2 LC)
Sl2 to CN, hold in front;
K2, K2 from CN

**Cable 2 over 2 Left,
Purl back (2/2 LPC)**
Sl2 to CN, hold in front;
P2, K2 from CN

Cable 2 over 2 Right (2/2 RC)
Sl2 to CN, hold in back;
K2, K2 from CN

**Cable 2 over 2 Right,
Purl back (2/2 RPC)**
Sl2 to CN, hold in back;
K2, P2 from CN

Bowline Hat

By Lee Meredith

Finished Measurements

16 (21)" circumference × 8.25 (9)" height, blocked; to fit head circumferences of 17–21 (22–25)"

Yarn

Wool of the Andes™ (worsted weight, 100% Peruvian Highland Wool; 110 yards/50g): Baltic Heather 25648, 2 skeins

Needles

US 6 (4mm) 16" circular needles and DPNs or two circular needles for two circulars technique or 32" or longer circular needles for Magic Loop technique, or size to obtain gauge

Notions

Yarn Needle
Stitch Marker(s)
Cable Needle

Gauge

26 sts and 28 rnds = 4" in 1x2 Rib in the round, blocked and unstretched (this is approximate due to the amount of stretch in the ribbing); stretches comfortably to approx 19 sts = 4"
24 sts and 28 rnds = 4" in cable pattern, blocked

This hat is designed to be a masterclass in cables! By the time any knitter is finished with it, they will be prepared to tackle any cabled project that crosses their path. Level up even more by trying the cables without a cable needle, and become a true cable-knitting expert!

Circumference can be adjusted a bit with blocking or by very slightly altering gauge. The smaller size is to fit children or small adult heads, while the larger size is for medium (with a semi-loose fit) or large adult heads. For medium adult heads and a more snug fit, choose the smaller size and stretch hard when blocking and/or go up one needle size from gauge needle.

Adjust height by adding to or subtracting from brim height. The body and crown are the same height for the two sizes—only the brim height differs, and it can be modified for personal preference. Work brim for 3–4 inches for a fold-up brim.

Always slip all stitches purlwise with yarn held to back.

Charts are worked in the round; read each chart row from right to left as a RS row.

K-YO-K (Knit, Yarn Over, Knit)
(K1, YO, K1) into 1 stitch.
2 sts inc.

RPT (Right Twist, Purl back)
Sl1 to CN, hold in back; K1, P1 from CN.

LPT (Left Twist, Purl back)
Sl1 to CN, hold in front; P1, K1 from CN.

RT (Right Twist)
Sl1 to CN, hold in back; K1, K1 from CN.

LT (Left Twist)
Sl1 to CN, hold in front; K1, K1 from CN.

1/2 RC (Cable 1 over 2 Right)
Sl2 to CN, hold in back; K1, K2 from CN.

2/1 RC (Cable 2 over 1 Right)
Sl1 to CN, hold in back; K2, K1 from CN.

3/3 RC (Cable 3 over 3 Right)
Sl3 to CN, hold in back; K3, K3 from CN.

4/2 RPC (Cable 4 over 2 Right, Purl back)
Sl2 to CN, hold in back; K4, P2 from CN.

4/2 RC (Cable 4 over 2 Right)
Sl2 to CN, hold in back; K4, K2 from CN.

2/2 RPC (Cable 2 over 2 Right, Purl back)
Sl2 to CN, hold in back; K2, P2 from CN.

2/2 LPC (Cable 2 over 2 Left, Purl back)
Sl2 to CN, hold in front; P2, K2 from CN.

2/2 RC (Cable 2 over 2 Right)
Sl2 to CN, hold in back; K2, K2 from CN.

2/2 LC (Cable 2 over 2 Left)
Sl2 to CN, hold in front; K2, K2 from CN.

LT-DecR (Left Twist, Decrease Right)
Sl1 to RH needle, Sl1 to CN, hold in front, Sl first st back to LH needle; K2tog, K1 from CN. 1 st dec.
or Sl1 to RH needle, twist next 2 sts on LH needle without a CN so that order is flipped in a left twist, Sl first st back to LH needle; K2tog, K1. 1 st dec.

LT-DecRL (Left Twist, Decrease 2 Right and Left)
Sl1 to RH needle, Sl1 to CN, hold in front, Sl first st back to LH needle; K2tog, Sl st from CN onto LH needle, SSK. 2 sts dec.
or Sl1 to RH needle, twist next 2 sts on LH needle without a CN so that order is flipped in a left twist, Sl first st back to LH needle; K2tog, SSK. 2 sts dec.

LT-DecL (Left Twist, Decrease Left)
Sl1 to CN, hold in front; K1, Sl1 st from CN onto LH needle, SSK. 1 st dec.
or Twist next 2 sts on LH needle without a CN so that order is flipped in a left twist; K1, SSK. 1 st dec.

1x2 RIB (in the round over a multiple of 3 sts)
All Rnds: (P2, K1) to end.

BOWLINE BODY (in the round beginning with a multiple of 27 sts)
Rnd 1: P2, K1, M1L, P2, K1, P2, K-YO-K, P2, K1, P2, M1R, (K1, P2) four times, K1. 4 sts inc.
Rnd 2: P2, K2, (P2, K1) two times, KFB, (K1, P2) two times, K2, (P2, K1) four times. 1 st inc. 32 sts.
Rnd 3: P2, Sl1, K1, P2, Sl1, P2, K4, P2, Sl1, P2, K1, Sl1, (P2, K1) four times.
Rnd 4: P2, RT, K3, P2, K4, P2, K3, LT, (P2, K4) two times.
Rnd 5: Rep Rnd 3.
Rnd 6: P2, RT, K1, RPT, P2, 2/2 LC, P2, LPT, K1, LT, (P2, K4) two times.
Rnd 7: P2, Sl1, K1, P1, Sl1, P3, K4, P3, Sl1, P1, K1, Sl1, (P2, K1) four times.
Rnd 8: P2, RT, RPT, P1, 2/2 RC, 2/2 LC, P1, LPT, LT, (P2, K4) two times.
Rnd 9: P2, Sl1, K1, Sl1, P2, K8, P2, Sl1, K1, Sl1, (P2, K1) four times.
Rnd 10: P2, K1, LT, P2, K8, P2, RT, K1, P2, K4, 4/2 RC.
Rnd 11: P2, K2, Sl1, P2, K8, P2, Sl1, K2, P2, K1, P2, K2, P2, K1, P1, K1.
Rnd 12: P2, RT, K1, P2, K8, P2, K1, LT, P2, K2, 4/2 RC, K2.
Rnd 13: P2, Sl1, K2, P2, K8, P2, K2, Sl1, P2, K1, P1, K1, P2, K2, P2, K1.
Rnd 14: P2, K1, LT, P2, K2, 2/2 LC, K2, P2, RT, K1, P2, 4/2 RPC, K4.
Rnd 15: P2, K2, Sl1, P2, K8, P2, Sl1, K2, (P2, K1) four times.
Rnd 16: P2, RT, K1, P2, (2/2 RC) two times, P2, K1, LT, (P2, K4) two times.
Rnd 17: P2, Sl1, K2, P2, K8, P2, K2, Sl1, (P2, K1) four times.
Rnd 18: P2, K1, LT, P2, K2, 2/2 LC, K2, P2, RT, K1, (P2, K4) two times.
Rnds 19–21: Rep Rnds 15–17.
Rnd 22: P2, K1, LT, P2, K2, 2/2 LC, K2, P2, RT, K1, P2, K4, 4/2 RC.
Rnds 23–25: Rep Rnds 11–13.

Rnd 26: P2, K1, LT, P2, K8, P2, RT, K1, P2, 4/2 RPC, K4.
Rnd 27: Rep Rnd 15.
Rnd 28: P2, RT, LT, P1, 2/2 LPC, 2/2 RPC, P1, RT, LT, (P2, K4) two times.
Rnd 29: P2, Sl1, K1, P1, Sl1, P3, K4, P3, Sl1, P1, K1, Sl1, (P2, K1) four times.
Rnd 30: P2, RT, K1, LT, P2, 2/2 LC, P2, RT, K1, LT, (P2, K4) two times.
Rnds 31–39: Rep Rnds 3–11.

BOWLINE CROWN (in the round beginning with a multiple of 32 sts)
Rnd 1: P2, RT, SSK, P1, K2tog, K4, SSK, P1, K2tog, LT, P2, K2, K3tog, K5. 6 sts dec.
Rnd 2: P2, Sl1, K2, P1, K6, P1, K2, Sl1, (P2, K1) two times.
Rnd 3: P2, K1, LT, P1, K1, 2/2 LC, K1, P1, RT, K1, P2, 4/2 RC, K2.
Rnd 4: P2, K2, Sl1, P1, K6, P1, Sl1, K2, P2, (K1, P2, K1) two times.
Rnd 5: P2, RT, K1, P1, 2/1 RC, 1/2 RC, P1, K1, LT, P2, K8.
Rnd 6: P2, Sl1, K2, P1, K6, P1, K2, Sl1, P2, (K1, P2, K1) two times.
Rnd 7: (P1, K2tog, LT) two times, SSK, P1, RT, SSK, P1, (K1, K2tog, K1) two times. 6 sts dec.
Rnd 8: P1, K2, Sl1, P1, K4, P1, Sl1, K2, P1, (K1, P1, K1) two times.
Rnd 9: P1, RT, K1, P1, (RT) two times, P1, K1, LT, P1, 3/3 RC.
Rnd 10: P1, Sl1, K2, P1, K4, P1, K2, Sl1, P1, (K1, P1, K1) two times.
Rnd 11: (P1, K1, LT) two times, K1, P1, RT, K1, P1, K6.
Rnd 12: P1, K2, Sl1, P1, K4, P1, Sl1, K2, P1, (K1, P1, K1) two times.
Rnd 13: P1, SSK, K1, P1, SSK, K2tog, P1, K1, SSK, P1, (K1, K2tog) two times. 6 sts dec.
Rnd 14: (P1, K1, Sl1, P1, K2) two times, K2.
Rnd 15: (P1, LT) three times, P1, 2/2 RC.
Rnd 16: (P1, K1, Sl1) three times, P1, K4.
Rnd 17: LT-decR, LT-decRL, LT-decL, (K2tog) two times. 6 sts dec. 8 sts remain.
Rnd 18: K8.
Rnd 19: (LT) four times.

Rnd 20: K8.
Rnd 21: (SSK) four times. 4 sts dec.

Directions

BRIM

CO 81 (108) sts. Join to work in the rnd, being careful not to twist sts, and PM for BOR.

Work 1x2 Rib (beginning rnd with P2) until piece measures 1.25 (2)" from CO edge. Optional: See *Notes* for adjusting height of brim.

BODY

Work Rnds 1–39 of Bowline Body from written instructions or chart, repeating cable pattern 3 (4) times around each rnd. (PMs between reps if desired.) *Note:* After Rnd 2 is complete, there are 96 (128) sts total.

CROWN

Work Rnds 1–21 of Bowline Crown from written instructions or chart, repeating pattern 3 (4) times around each rnd. (If using 16" circular needle, switch to DPNs when necessary to accommodate number of sts.)

Break yarn and use yarn needle to thread tail through remaining 12 (16) sts. Pull tight to close hole and fasten.

FINISHING

Weave in ends, wash, and block as you like. Hat can be stretched out larger when blocking, or stay unstretched for a stretchier fit when wearing, depending on finished size and fit preferences.

No Stitch
Placeholder—no stitch made

Knit Stitch

Purl Stitch

Sl
Slip stitch purl-wise, with yarn in back

M1R
Make 1 right-leaning stitch

M1L
Make 1 left-leaning stitch

KFB
Knit into the front and back of the stitch

K-YO-K
(Knit 1, Yarn Over, Knit 1) into 1 stitch

Right Twist (RT)
Sl1 to CN, hold in back; K1, K1 from CN

Left Twist (LT)
Sl1 to CN, hold in front; K1, K1 from CN

Right Twist, Purl back (RPT)
Sl1 to CN, hold in back; K1, P1 from CN

Left Twist, Purl back (LPT)
Sl1 to CN, hold in front; P1, K1 from CN

Cable 2 over 2 Right (2/2 RC)
Sl2 to CN, hold in back; K2,
K2 from CN

Cable 2 over 2 Left (2/2 LC)
Sl2 to CN, hold in front; K2,
K2 from CN

**Cable 2 over 2 Right, Purl back
(2/2 RPC)**
Sl2 to CN, hold in back; K2,
P2 from CN

**Cable 2 over 2 Left, Purl back
(2/2 LPC)**
Sl2 to CN, hold in front; P2,
K2 from CN

Cable 4 over 2 Right (4/2 RC)
Sl2 to CN, hold in back; K4,
K2 from CN

**Cable 4 over 2 Right, Purl
back (4/2 RPC)**
Sl2 to CN, hold in back; K4,
P2 from CN

BOWLINE BODY

BOWLINE CROWN

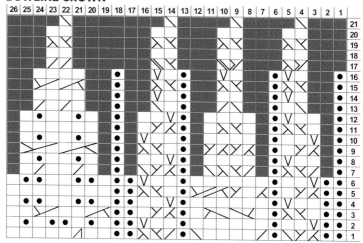

K2tog
Knit 2 stitches together as one stitch

SSK
Slip, slip, knit slipped stitches together

K3tog
Knit 3 stitches together as one stitch

Cable 3 over 3 Right (3/3 RC)
Sl3 to CN, hold in back; K3, K3 from CN

Cable 2 over 1 Right (2/1 RC)
Sl1 to CN, hold in back; K2, K1 from CN

Cable 1 over 2 Right (1/2 RC)
Sl2 to CN, hold in back; K1, K2 from CN

Left Twist, Decrease Right (LT-decR)
Sl1 to RH needle, Sl1 to CN, hold in front, Sl first st back to LH needle; K2tog, K1 from CN

Left Twist, Decrease 2 Right/Left (LT-decRL)
Sl1 to RH needle, Sl1 to CN, hold in front, Sl first st back to LH needle; K2tog, Sl st from CN onto LH needle, SSK

Left Twist, Decrease Left (LT-decL)
Sl1 to CN, hold in front; SSK, K1 from CN

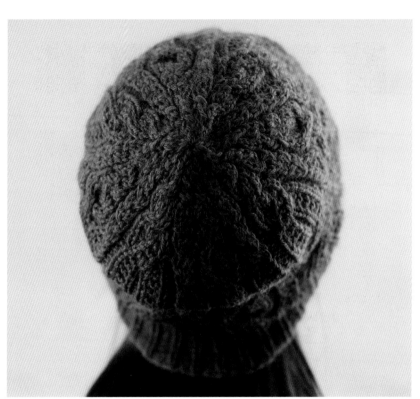

Tuckamore Wrap

By Katie Noseworthy

Finished Measurements
19.5" width × 73.75" length

Yarn
Wool of the Andes™ Tweed
(worsted weight, 80% Peruvian
Highland Wool, 20% Donegal
Tweed; 110 yards/50g): Down
Heather 25458, 13 skeins

Needles
US 7 (4.5mm) straight or 24"
circular needles, or size to obtain
gauge
US 6 (4mm) straight or 24" circular
needles, or one size smaller than
size used to obtain gauge

Notions
Yarn Needle
Stitch Markers
Cable Needles
Blocking Wires (optional)

Gauge
24 sts and 24 rows = 4" in
Cable Pattern with larger
needles, blocked

Tuckamore is a large, rectangular wrap inspired by foliage of the same name that can be found in western Newfoundland, Canada. The unique phenomenon is caused by the relentless wind, stunting the growth of trees to form gnarled and closely matted ground cover on the barrens. This intricate design draws inspiration from the tangled branches and resilience of nature, to create a thick, warm wrap, suitable for the cold northern winter.

Tuckamore is worked flat from end to end with three cabled panels running along its length—traditional plaits and diamonds border a central panel of winding, Celtic knots that illustrate the essence of its namesake.

Included are both charted and written instructions. Charts are worked flat; read RS rows (odd numbers) from right to left, and WS rows (even numbers) from left to right. Cable crosses are only worked on RS rows.

2/2 LC (Cable 2 over 2 Left)
Sl2 to CN, hold in front; K2, K2 from CN.

2/2 RC (Cable 2 over 2 Right)
Sl2 to CN, hold in back; K2, K2 from CN.

2/1 LPC (Cable 2 over 1 Left, Purl back)
Sl2 to CN, hold in front; P1, K2 from CN.

2/1 RPC (Cable 2 over 1 Right, Purl back)
Sl1 to CN, hold in back; K2, P1 from CN.

3/3 LC (Cable 3 over 3 Left)
Sl3 to CN, hold in front; K3, K3 from CN.

3/3 RC (Cable 3 over 3 Right)
Sl3 to CN, hold in back; K3, K3 from CN.

3/2 LPC (Cable 3 over 2 Left, Purl back)
Sl3 to CN, hold in front; P2, K3 from CN.

3/2 RPC (Cable 3 over 2 Right, Purl back)
Sl2 to CN, hold in back; K3, P2 from CN.

2/1/2 LC (Cable 2 over 2 Left, Purl 1 center back)
Sl3 to CN, hold in front; K2, Sl1 from CN back onto LH needle, K1, K2 from CN.

2/1/2 RC (Cable 2 over 2 Right, Purl 1 center back)
Sl3 to CN, hold in back; K2, Sl1 from CN back onto LH needle, K1, K2 from CN.

SEED STITCH BORDER (worked flat over a multiple of 2 sts plus 1)
Row 1: (K1, P1) to last st, K1.
Rep Row 1 for pattern.

PATTERN A (worked flat over 29 sts)
Row 1 (RS): K2, 2/2 RC, K2, P5, 2/1/2 RC, P5, 2/2 RC, K2.
Row 2 (WS): P6, K5, P5, K5, P6, K2.
Row 3: K4, 2/2 LC, P4, 2/1 RPC, K1, 2/1 LPC, P4, K2, 2/2 LC.
Row 4: P6, K4, P2, K1, P1, K1, P2, K4, P6, K2.
Row 5: K2, 2/2 RC, K2, P3, 2/1 RPC, K1, P1, K1, 2/1 LPC, P3, 2/2 RC, K2.
Row 6: P6, K3, P2, (K1, P1) two times, K1, P2, K3, P6, K2.
Row 7: K4, 2/2 LC, P2, 2/1 RPC, (K1, P1) two times, K1, 2/1 LPC, P2, K2, 2/2 LC.
Row 8: P6, K2, P2, (K1, P1) three times, K1, P2, K2, P6, K2.
Row 9: K2, 2/2 RC, K2, P1, 2/1 RPC, (K1, P1) three times, K1, 2/1 LPC, P1, 2/2 RC, K2.
Row 10: P6, K1, P2, (K1, P1) four times, K1, P2, K1, P6, K2.
Row 11: K4, 2/2 LC, P1, K3, (P1, K1) three times, P1, K3, P1, K2, 2/2 LC.
Row 12: P6, K1, P3, (K1, P1) three times, K1, P3, K1, P6, K2.
Row 13: K2, 2/2 RC, K2, P1, K2, (P1, K1) four times, P1, K2, P1, 2/2 RC, K2.
Row 14: P6, K1, P2, (K1, P1) four times, K1, P2, K1, P6, K2.

Row 15: K4, 2/2 LC, P1, 2/1 LPC, (P1, K1) three times, P1, 2/1 RPC, P1, K2 2/2 LC.
Row 16: P6, K2, P2, (K1, P1) three times, K1, P2, K2, P6, K2.
Row 17: K2, 2/2 RC, K2, P2, 2/1 LPC, (P1, K1) two times, P1, 2/1 RPC, P2, 2/2 RC, K2.
Row 18: P6, K3, P2, (K1, P1) two times, K1, P2, K3, P6, K2.
Row 19: K4, 2/2 LC, P3, 2/1 LPC, P1, K1, P1, 2/1 RPC, P3, K2, 2/2 LC.
Row 20: P6, K4, P2, K1, P1, K1, P2, K4, P6, K2.
Row 21: K2, 2/2 RC, K2, P4, 2/1 LPC, P1, 2/1 RPC, P4, 2/2 RC, K2.
Row 22: P6, K5, P2, K1, P2, K5, P6, K2.
Row 23: K4, 2/2 LC, P5, 2/1/2 RC, P5, K2, 2/2 LC.
Row 24: P6, K5, P5, K5, P6, K2.
Rep Rows 1–24 for pattern.

PATTERN B (worked flat over 59 sts)
Row 1 (RS): P2, K3, P4, (3/3 LC, P4) five times.
Row 2 (WS): (K4, P6) five times, K4, P3, K2.
Row 3: P2, (3/2 LPC, 3/2 RPC) five times, 3/2 LPC, P2.
Row 4: K2, P3, K4 (P6, K4) five times.
Row 5: (P4, 3/3 RC) five times, P4, K3, P2.
Row 6: K2, P3, K4 (P6, K4) five times.
Row 7: P2 (3/2 RPC, 3/2 LPC) five times, 3/2 RPC, P2.
Row 8: (K4, P6) five times, K4, P3, K2.
Rep Rows 1–8 for pattern.

PATTERN C (worked flat over 29 sts)
Row 1 (RS): K2, 2/2 LC, P5, 2/1/2 LC, P5, K2, 2/2 LC, K2.
Row 2 (WS): K2, P6, K5, P5, K5, P6.
Row 3: 2/2 RC, K2, P4, 2/1 RPC, K1, 2/1 LPC, P4, 2/2 RC, K4.
Row 4: K2, P6, K4, P2, K1, P1, K1, P2, K4, P6.
Row 5: K2, 2/2 LC, P3, 2/1 RPC, K1, P1, K1, 2/1 LPC, P3, K2, 2/2 LC, K2.
Row 6: K2, P6, K3, P2, (K1, P1) two times, K1, P2, K3, P6.
Row 7: 2/2 RC, K2, P2, 2/1 RPC, (K1, P1) two times, K1, 2/1 LPC, P2, 2/2 RC, K4.

Row 8: K2, P6, K2, P2, (K1, P1) three times, K1, P2, K2, P6.
Row 9: K2, 2/2 LC, P1, 2/1 RPC, (K1, P1) three times, K1, 2/1 LPC, P1, K2, 2/2 LC, K2.
Row 10: K2, P6, K1, P2, (K1, P1) four times, K1, P2, K1, P6.
Row 11: 2/2 RC, K2, P1, K3, (P1, K1) three times, P1, K3, P1, 2/2 RC, K4.
Row 12: K2, P6, K1, P3, (K1, P1) three times, K1, P3, K1, P6.
Row 13: K2, 2/2 LC, P1, K2, (P1, K1) four times, P1, K2, P1, K2, 2/2 LC, K2.
Row 14: K2, P6, K1, P2, (K1, P1) four times, K1, P2, K1, P6.
Row 15: 2/2 RC, K2, P1, 2/1 LPC, (P1, K1) three times, P1, 2/1 RPC, P1, 2/2 RC, K4.
Row 16: K2, P6, K2, P2, (K1, P1) three times, K1, P2, K2, P6.
Row 17: K2, 2/2 LC, P2, 2/1 LPC, (P1, K1) two times, P1, 2/1 RPC, P2, K2, 2/2 LC, K2.
Row 18: K2, P6, K3, P2, (K1, P1) two times, K1, P2, K3, P6.
Row 19: 2/2 RC, K2, P3, 2/1 LPC, P1, K1, P1, 2/1 RPC, P3, 2/2 RC, K4.
Row 20: K2, P6, K4, P2, K1, P1, K1, P2, K4, P6.
Row 21: K2, 2/2 LC, P4, 2/1 LPC, P1, 2/1 RPC, P4, K2, 2/2 LC, K2.
Row 22: K2, P6, K5, P2, K1, P2, K5, P6.
Row 23: 2/2 RC, K2, P5, 2/1/2 LC, P5, 2/2 RC, K4.
Row 24: K2, P6, K5, P5, K5, P6.
Rep Rows 1–24 for pattern.

Directions

BEGINNING BORDER

Using smaller needles, CO 117 sts.
Work Seed Stitch Border for five rows.

Switch to larger needles.
Cable Set Up Row (WS): K2, P6, K5, P5, K5,
P6, PM, (K4, P6) five times, K4, P3, K2, PM,
P6, K5, P5, K5, P6, K2.

BODY

Body Rows can be worked using either
the charts or written instructions.

Row 1 (RS): Work Pattern A, SM, work
Pattern B, SM, work Pattern C.
Row 2 (WS): Work Pattern C, SM, work
Pattern B, SM, work Pattern A.
Rep Rows 1–2 until Rows 1–24 of Patterns A
and C have been worked a total of 18 times.

ENDING BORDER

Switch to smaller needles.
Work Seed Stitch Border for five rows.

BO loosely in pattern to allow for stretch
during blocking.

FINISHING

Weave in ends, wash, and block.
Blocking wires are recommended to keep
the edges straight.

K
RS: Knit stitch
WS: Purl stitch

P
RS: Purl stitch
WS: Knit stitch

Cable 2 over 1 Right, Purl back (2/1 RPC)
Sl1 to CN, hold in back; K2, P1 from CN

Cable 2 over 1 Left, Purl back (2/1 LPC)
Sl2 to CN, hold in front; P1, K2 from CN

Cable 2 over 2 Right (2/2 RC)
Sl2 to CN, hold in back; K2, K2 from CN

Cable 2 over 2 Left (2/2 LC)
Sl2 to CN, hold in front; K2, K2 from CN

Cable 3 over 2 Right, Purl back (3/2 RPC)
Sl2 to CN, hold in back; K3, P2 from CN

Cable 3 over 2 Left, Purl back (3/2 LPC)
Sl3 to CN, hold in front; P2, K3 from CN

Cable 2 over 2 Right, Purl 1 center back (2/1/2 RC)
Sl3 to CN, hold in back; K2, Sl last st from CN
back to left-hand needle and knit it; K2 from CN

Cable 2 over 2 Left, Purl 1 center back (2/1/2 LC)
Sl3 to CN, hold in front; K2, Sl last st from CN
back to left-hand needle and knit it; K2 from CN

Cable 3 over 3 Right (3/3 RC)
Sl3 to CN, hold in back; K3, K3 from CN

Cable 3 over 3 Left (3/3 LC)
Sl3 to CN, hold in front; K3, K3 from CN

Pattern Repeat

PATTERN A

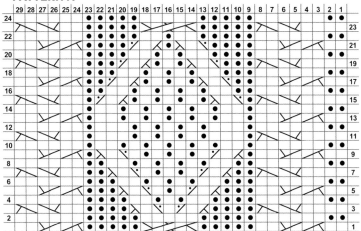

PATTERN B

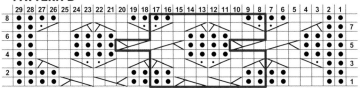

rep red boxed sts four times

PATTERN C

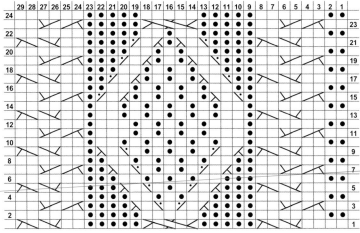

Glossary

Slipped Stitches (Sl)

Always slip stitches purl-wise with yarn held to the wrong side of work, unless noted otherwise in the pattern.

Make 1 Left-Leaning Stitch (M1L)

Inserting LH needle from front to back, PU the horizontal strand between the st just worked and the next st, and K TBL.

Make 1 Right-Leaning Stitch (M1R)

Inserting LH needle from back to front, PU the horizontal strand between the st just worked and the next st, and K TFL.

Slip, Slip, Knit (SSK)

(Sl1 K-wise) twice; insert LH needle into front of these 2 sts and knit them together.

Centered Double Decrease (CDD)

Slip first and second sts together as if to work K2tog; K1; pass 2 slipped sts over the knit st.

Stockinette Stitch
(St st, flat over any number of sts)

Row 1 (RS): Knit all sts.
Row 2 (WS): Purl all sts.
Rep Rows 1–2 for pattern.
St st in the round: Knit every rnd.
Rev St st: Purl on RS, knit on WS.

Long Tail Cast On

A good, basic cast on option for most projects. A tutorial can be found at knitpicks.com/learning-center/learn-to-knit.

Knitting in the Round

Photo and video tutorials for several methods can be found at knitpicks.com/learning-center/knitting-in-round.

Mattress Stitch

A neat, invisible seaming method for joining two edges together. A tutorial can be found at tutorials.knitpicks.com/mattress-stitch.

ABBREVIATIONS

approx	approximately	M1R *(inc 1)*	make 1 right-leaning stitch *(see above)*	Sl	slip *(see above)*
BO	bind off			SM	slip marker
BOR	beginning of round	P	purl	SSK *(dec 1)*	slip, slip, knit these 2 stitches together *(see above)*
CN	cable needle	P2tog *(dec 1)*	purl 2 stitches together		
CDD *(dec 2)*	centered double decrease *(see above)*	P3tog *(dec 2)*	purl 3 stitches together	SSP *(dec 1)*	slip, slip, purl these 2 stitches together through back loop
CO	cast on	PM	place marker		
cont	continue	PFB *(inc 1)*	purl into front and back of stitch	SSSK *(dec 2)*	slip, slip, slip, knit these 3 stitches together (like SSK)
dec(s)	decrease(es)				
DPN(s)	double pointed needle(s)	PSSO *(dec 1)*	pass slipped stitch over	St st	stockinette stitch *(see above)*
inc(s)	increase(s)	PU	pick up	st(s)	stitch(es)
K	knit	P-wise	purl-wise	TBL	through back loop
K2tog *(dec 1)*	knit 2 stitches together	rep	repeat	TFL	through front loop
K3tog *(dec 2)*	knit 3 stitches together	Rev St st	reverse stockinette stitch *(see above)*	tog	together
KFB *(inc 1)*	knit into front and back of stitch	RH	right hand	W&T	wrap & turn
		rnd(s)	round(s)	WE	work even
K-wise	knit-wise	RS	right side	WS	wrong side
LH	left hand	SK2P *(dec 2)*	slip 1 knit-wise, knit 2 together, pass slipped stitch over	WYIB	with yarn in back
M	marker			WYIF	with yarn in front
M1L *(inc 1)*	make 1 left-leaning stitch *(see above)*	SKP *(dec 1)*	slip k-wise, knit, pass slipped stitch over	YO *(inc 1)*	bring yarn over needle from front up over to back